# Simple 1-2-3™
# Chicken

Publications International, Ltd.

**Pictured on the front cover:** Sesame Chicken *(page 73)*.

**Pictured on the back cover** *(top to bottom):* Sausage and Chicken Gumbo *(page 24)* and Blackened Chicken Salad in Pitas *(page 56)*.

ISBN-13: 978-1-60553-118-2
ISBN-10: 1-60553-118-9

Library of Congress Control Number: 2009932726

Manufactured in China.

8 7 6 5 4 3 2 1

**Preparation/Cooking Times:** Preparation times are based on the approximate amount of time required to assemble the recipe before cooking, baking, chilling or serving. These times include preparation steps such as measuring, chopping and mixing. The fact that some preparations and cooking can be done simultaneously is taken into account. Preparation of optional ingredients and serving suggestions is not included.

Publications International, Ltd.

# Contents

# Easy Appetizers

## Tortilla "Pizzas"

1 can (about 14 ounces) Mexican-style stewed tomatoes, drained
1 can (10 ounces) chunk white chicken packed in water, drained
1 green onion, minced
2 teaspoons ground cumin, divided
½ teaspoon garlic powder
1 cup refried beans
4 tablespoons chopped fresh cilantro, divided
2 large or 4 small flour tortillas
1 cup (4 ounces) shredded Monterey Jack cheese with jalapeño
    peppers

**1.** Preheat broiler. Combine tomatoes, chicken, green onion, 1 teaspoon cumin and garlic powder in medium bowl. Combine refried beans, remaining 1 teaspoon cumin and 2 tablespoons cilantro in small bowl.

**2.** Place tortillas on baking sheet. Broil 30 seconds per side or until crisp but not browned. Remove from oven. *Reduce oven temperature to 400°F.* Spread bean mixture evenly over each tortilla. Top with chicken mixture and cheese. Bake 5 minutes.

**3.** *Turn oven to broil.* Broil tortillas 2 to 3 minutes or until cheese melts. *Do not let tortilla edges burn.* Top with remaining 2 tablespoons cilantro. *Makes 8 servings*

**Serving Suggestion:** Serve with a green salad tossed with avocado and a lemon vinaigrette.

Prep and Cook Time: 19 minutes

# Apricot-Chicken Pot Stickers

**2 cups plus 1 tablespoon water, divided**
**2 boneless skinless chicken breasts**
**2 cups chopped finely shredded cabbage**
**½ cup apricot fruit spread**
**2 green onions, finely chopped**
**2 teaspoons reduced-sodium soy sauce**
**½ teaspoon grated fresh ginger**
**⅛ teaspoon black pepper**
**30 (3-inch) wonton wrappers**
**Prepared sweet and sour sauce (optional)**

**1.** Bring 2 cups water to a boil in medium saucepan. Add chicken. Reduce heat to low; cover and simmer 10 minutes or until chicken is no longer pink in center. Drain chicken; remove from saucepan.

**2.** Place cabbage and remaining 1 tablespoon water in same saucepan. Cook and stir over high heat 1 to 2 minutes or until water evaporates. Remove from heat; cool slightly. Finely chop chicken. Return chicken to saucepan with cabbage. Add fruit spread, green onions, soy sauce, ginger and pepper; mix well.

**3.** To assemble pot stickers, remove 3 wonton wrappers at a time from package. Spoon slightly rounded tablespoonful chicken mixture onto center of each wrapper; brush edges of wrapper with water. Bring 4 corners together; press to seal. Repeat with remaining wrappers and filling.

**4.** Spray steamer with nonstick cooking spray. Assemble steamer with water up to ½ inch below steamer basket. Fill basket with pot stickers, leaving enough space between to prevent sticking. Cover; steam 5 minutes. Serve with sweet and sour sauce, if desired.

*Makes 10 servings*

# Chicken Tortilla Roll-Ups

4 ounces cream cheese, softened
2 tablespoons mayonnaise
1 tablespoon Dijon mustard
¼ teaspoon black pepper
3 (10- or 12-inch) flour tortillas
1 cup finely chopped cooked
　chicken
¾ cup shredded or finely chopped
　carrot
¾ cup finely chopped green bell
　pepper
3 tablespoons chopped green
　onions

**1.** Combine cream cheese, mayonnaise, mustard and black pepper in small bowl; stir until well blended.

**2.** Spread cream cheese mixture evenly onto each tortilla, leaving ½-inch border. Sprinkle chicken, carrot, bell pepper and green onions evenly over cream cheese, leaving 1½-inch border on cream cheese mixture at one end of each tortilla.

**3.** Roll up each tortilla jelly-roll fashion. Cut rolls into 1½-inch-thick slices.                    *Makes about 18 slices*

**Note:** Wrap rolls in plastic wrap and refrigerate for several hours for easier slicing and to allow flavors to blend.

# Coconut Chicken Tenders with Spicy Mango Salsa

1 ripe mango, chopped
½ cup diced red bell pepper
3 tablespoons thinly sliced green onions
2 tablespoons minced fresh cilantro
Salt and ground red pepper
1½ cups flaked coconut
1 egg
1 tablespoon vegetable oil
¾ pound chicken tenders

**1.** Combine mango, bell pepper, green onions and cilantro in small bowl. Season to taste with salt and ground red pepper. Transfer half of salsa to food processor; process until finely chopped (almost puréed). Combine with remaining salsa.

**2.** Preheat oven to 400°F. Spread coconut on large baking sheet; bake 5 to 6 minutes or until lightly browned, stirring every 2 minutes. Transfer coconut to food processor; process until finely chopped but not pasty.

**3.** Beat egg with oil and pinch of ground red pepper in medium bowl. Add chicken tenders; toss to coat. Roll tenders in coconut; arrange on foil-lined baking sheet. Bake 18 to 20 minutes or until no longer pink in center. Serve with Spicy Mango Salsa. *Makes 5 to 6 servings*

# Chicken Empanadas

**4 ounces cream cheese**
**2 tablespoons minced fresh cilantro**
**2 tablespoons salsa**
**½ teaspoon salt**
**½ teaspoon ground cumin**
**¼ teaspoon garlic powder**
**1 cup finely chopped cooked chicken**
**1 package (about 15 ounces) refrigerated pie crusts (2 crusts),**
     **at room temperature**
**1 egg, beaten**
     **Additional salsa (optional)**

**1.** Heat cream cheese in medium saucepan over low heat, stirring constantly, until melted. Add cilantro, salsa, salt, cumin and garlic powder; stir until smooth. Stir in chicken; remove from heat.

**2.** Preheat oven to 425°F. Line 2 baking sheets with parchment paper or foil. Roll out pie crust dough on lightly floured surface. Cut dough with 3-inch round cutter. Reroll dough scraps and cut out rounds. Place about 2 teaspoons chicken mixture in center of each dough round. Brush edges lightly with water. Fold one side of dough over filling to form half circle; pinch edges to seal.

**3.** Arrange empanadas on prepared baking sheets; brush lightly with egg. Bake 16 to 18 minutes or until lightly browned. Serve with additional salsa, if desired.                                *Makes 10 servings*

**Note:** Empanadas can be prepared ahead of time and frozen. Simply wrap unbaked empanadas in foil and freeze. To bake, unwrap and follow directions in step 3, baking 18 to 20 minutes.

# Grilled Chicken Tostadas

1 pound boneless skinless chicken breasts
1 teaspoon ground cumin
¼ cup plus 2 tablespoons salsa, divided
¼ cup orange juice
1 tablespoon plus 2 teaspoons vegetable oil, divided
2 cloves garlic, minced
8 green onions
1 can (16 ounces) refried beans
4 (10-inch) or 8 (6- to 7-inch) flour tortillas
2 cups chopped romaine lettuce
1½ cups (6 ounces) shredded Monterey Jack cheese
1 ripe medium avocado, diced
1 medium tomato, seeded and diced
Chopped fresh cilantro and sour cream (optional)

**1.** Place chicken in single layer in shallow glass dish; sprinkle with cumin. Combine ¼ cup salsa, orange juice, 1 tablespoon oil and garlic in small bowl; pour over chicken. Cover; marinate in refrigerator at least 2 hours or up to 8 hours, stirring occasionally.

**2.** Prepare grill for direct cooking. Drain chicken; reserve marinade. Brush green onions with remaining 2 teaspoons oil. Grill, covered, over medium-high heat 5 minutes. Brush tops of chicken with half of reserved marinade; turn and brush with remaining marinade. Turn onions. Grill, covered, 5 minutes more or until chicken is no longer pink in center and onions are tender. Place tortillas in single layer on grid. Grill, uncovered, 1 to 2 minutes per side or until golden brown.

**3.** Meanwhile, combine beans and remaining 2 tablespoons salsa in small saucepan. Cook over medium heat, stirring occasionally, until hot.

**4.** Transfer chicken and onions to cutting board. Slice chicken crosswise into ½-inch strips. Cut onions crosswise into 1-inch-long pieces. Spread tortillas with bean mixture; top with lettuce, chicken, onions, cheese, avocado and tomato. Sprinkle with cilantro and serve with sour cream, if desired. *Makes 4 servings*

# Honey-Sauced Chicken Wings

**3 pounds chicken wings**
**1 teaspoon salt**
**½ teaspoon black pepper**
**1 cup honey**
**½ cup soy sauce**
**¼ cup chopped onion**
**¼ cup ketchup**
**2 tablespoons vegetable oil**
**2 cloves garlic, minced**
**¼ teaspoon red pepper flakes**
   **Sesame seeds, toasted***
   **(optional)**

*\*To toast sesame seeds, spread seeds in small skillet. Shake skillet over medium-low heat 3 minutes or until seeds begin to pop and turn golden.*

SLOW COOKER DIRECTIONS

**1.** Preheat broiler. Remove and discard wing tips. Cut each wing in half at joint. Sprinkle chicken with salt and black pepper; place on broiler pan. Broil 4 to 5 inches from heat 20 minutes or until chicken is browned, turning once. Transfer chicken to slow cooker.

**2.** Combine honey, soy sauce, onion, ketchup, oil, garlic and pepper flakes in medium bowl. Pour over chicken.

**3.** Cover; cook on LOW 4 to 5 hours or on HIGH 2 to 2½ hours. Garnish with sesame seeds. *Makes about 32 appetizers*

# Chicken Wraps

½ **pound boneless skinless chicken thighs**
½ **teaspoon Chinese five-spice powder**
½ **cup bean sprouts**
2 **tablespoons minced green onion**
2 **tablespoons sliced almonds**
2 **tablespoons reduced-sodium soy sauce**
4 **teaspoons hoisin sauce**
1 to 2 **teaspoons chili garlic sauce***
4 **large lettuce leaves**

*Chili garlic sauce is available in the Asian foods section of most large supermarkets.*

**1.** Preheat oven to 350°F. Place chicken on baking sheet; sprinkle with five-spice powder. Bake 20 minutes or until chicken is cooked through. Set aside to cool.

**2.** Dice chicken. Combine chicken, bean sprouts, green onion, almonds, soy sauce, hoisin sauce and chili garlic sauce in large bowl.

**3.** To serve, spoon ⅓ cup chicken mixture onto each lettuce leaf; roll or fold as desired. *Makes 4 servings*

# Garlicky Gilroy Chicken Wings

    1 cup olive oil, plus additional to grease pan
    2 pounds chicken wings
    2 heads fresh garlic, separated into cloves and peeled*
    1 teaspoon hot pepper sauce, or to taste
    1 cup grated Parmesan cheese
    1 cup Italian-style dry bread crumbs
    1 teaspoon black pepper
    Carrot and celery slices (optional)

*To peel whole heads of garlic, drop into boiling water for 5 to 10 seconds. Immediately remove garlic with slotted spoon. Plunge garlic into cold water; drain. Peel away skins.*

**1.** Preheat oven to 375°F. Grease 13×9-inch nonstick baking pan. Remove and discard wing tips. Cut each wing in half at joint.

**2.** Place garlic, 1 cup oil and hot pepper sauce in food processor; process until smooth. Pour garlic mixture into small bowl. Combine cheese, bread crumbs and black pepper in shallow dish. Dip chicken, 1 wing at a time, into garlic mixture, then roll in crumb mixture, coating evenly and shaking off excess.

**3.** Arrange chicken in single layer in prepared pan. Drizzle remaining garlic mixture over chicken; sprinkle with remaining crumb mixture. Bake 45 to 60 minutes or until chicken is browned and crisp. Serve with carrot and celery slices, if desired.          *Makes about 6 servings*

# Chicken-Pesto Pizza

**½ pound chicken tenders**
**1 medium onion, thinly sliced**
**⅓ cup prepared pesto**
**3 medium plum tomatoes, thinly sliced**
**1 (14-inch) prepared pizza crust**
**1 cup (4 ounces) shredded mozzarella cheese**

**1.** Preheat oven to 450°F. Cut chicken tenders into bite-size pieces. Coat medium nonstick skillet with nonstick cooking spray; cook and stir chicken over medium heat 2 minutes. Add onion and pesto; cook and stir about 3 minutes or until chicken is cooked through.

**2.** Arrange tomato slices and chicken mixture on pizza crust, leaving 1-inch border. Sprinkle with cheese.

**3.** Bake 8 minutes or until pizza is hot and cheese is melted and bubbly.

*Makes 6 servings*

Prep and Cook Time: 22 minutes

# Dijon Chicken Skewers

1 cup barbecue sauce
¼ cup yellow mustard
1 pound chicken tenders
Salt and black pepper

**1.** Soak 10 to 12 (10- to 12-inch) wooden skewers 20 minutes in cold water to prevent them from scorching; drain. Preheat broiler.

**2.** Combine barbecue sauce and mustard in medium bowl. Weave chicken tenders onto skewers; season with salt and pepper. Brush skewers with sauce mixture; coat well. Discard any remaining sauce.

**3.** Broil skewers 3 minutes. Turn and broil 3 to 5 minutes more or until chicken is no longer pink in center.

*Makes 10 to 12 skewers*

Prep Time: 20 minutes • Cook Time: about 10 minutes

# Simple Soups & Stews

## Main-Dish Chicken Soup

  1 tablespoon olive oil
  1 cup grated carrots
 ½ cup diced red bell pepper
 ½ cup sliced green onions
  6 cups chicken broth
 ½ cup frozen green peas
  1 seedless cucumber
12 chicken tenders (about 1 pound), halved
 ½ teaspoon white pepper

**1.** Heat oil in large saucepan over medium heat. Add carrots, bell pepper and green onions; cook and stir 2 minutes. Add broth and peas; bring to a boil. Reduce heat; simmer 2 minutes.

**2.** Meanwhile, cut ends off cucumber and discard. Using vegetable peeler, start at top and make long, noodle-like strips of cucumber. Cut any remaining cucumber pieces into thin slices. Add cucumber to saucepan; cook 2 minutes over low heat.

**3.** Add chicken tenders and white pepper; simmer 5 minutes or until chicken is cooked through. *Makes 6 servings*

**Serving Suggestion:** Serve with a small mixed green salad and crusty French bread.

# Tuscan Chicken with White Beans

**1 large bulb fennel (about ¾ pound)**
**1 teaspoon olive oil**
**1 teaspoon dried rosemary**
**½ teaspoon black pepper**
**½ pound boneless skinless chicken thighs, cut into ¾-inch pieces**
**1 can (about 14 ounces) stewed tomatoes**
**2 cups chicken broth**
**1 can (about 15 ounces) cannellini beans, rinsed and drained**
**Hot pepper sauce (optional)**

**1.** Cut off and reserve ¼ cup chopped feathery fennel tops, if desired. Chop bulb into ½-inch pieces. Heat oil in large saucepan over medium heat. Add chopped fennel bulb; cook and stir 5 minutes.

**2.** Sprinkle rosemary and pepper over chicken. Add to saucepan; cook and stir 2 minutes. Add tomatoes and broth; bring to a boil. Reduce heat; cover and simmer 10 minutes. Stir in beans; simmer, uncovered, 15 minutes or until chicken is cooked through and sauce has thickened.

**3.** Season to taste with hot pepper sauce. Ladle into 4 shallow bowls; garnish with reserved fennel tops. *Makes 4 servings*

Prep Time: 15 minutes • Cook Time: 35 minutes

# Thai Noodle Soup

1 package (3 ounces) ramen
   noodles
¾ pound chicken tenders
3½ cups chicken broth
¼ cup shredded carrot
¼ cup frozen snow peas
2 tablespoons thinly sliced green
   onion
½ teaspoon minced garlic
¼ teaspoon ground ginger
3 tablespoons chopped fresh
   cilantro
½ lime, cut into 4 wedges

**1.** Break noodles into pieces. Cook noodles according to package directions; discard flavor packet. Drain; set aside.

**2.** Cut chicken into ½-inch pieces. Combine chicken and broth in large saucepan. Bring to a boil over medium heat; cook 2 minutes.

**3.** Add carrot, snow peas, green onion, garlic and ginger. Reduce heat to low; simmer 3 minutes or until chicken is cooked through. Add cooked noodles and cilantro; heat through. Serve soup with lime wedges.

*Makes 4 servings*

Prep and Cook Time: 15 minutes

# Sausage and Chicken Gumbo

**1 tablespoon canola oil**
**1 red bell pepper, diced**
**1 pound boneless skinless chicken thighs, cut into 1-inch pieces**
**1 package (12 ounces) Cajun andouille or spicy chicken sausage,**
     **sliced ½ inch thick**
**½ cup chicken broth**
**1 can (28 ounces) crushed tomatoes with roasted garlic**
**¼ cup finely chopped green onions**
**1 bay leaf**
**½ teaspoon dried basil**
**½ teaspoon black pepper**
**¼ to ½ teaspoon red pepper flakes**
**6 lemon wedges (optional)**

**1.** Heat oil in large saucepan over medium-high heat. Add bell pepper; cook and stir 2 to 3 minutes. Add chicken; cook and stir about 2 minutes or until browned.

**2.** Add sausage; cook and stir 2 minutes or until browned. Add broth; scrape up any browned bits from bottom of saucepan.

**3.** Add tomatoes, green onions, bay leaf, basil, black pepper and pepper flakes. Simmer 15 minutes or until chicken is cooked through. Remove and discard bay leaf. Serve with lemon wedges, if desired.

*Makes 6 servings*

# Confetti Chicken Chili

  1 pound ground chicken
  1 large onion, chopped
 3½ cups chicken broth
  1 can (about 15 ounces) Great Northern beans, rinsed and drained
  2 carrots, chopped
  1 medium green bell pepper, diced
  2 plum tomatoes, chopped
  1 jalapeño pepper,* finely chopped (optional)
  2 teaspoons chili powder
  ½ teaspoon ground red pepper

*Jalapeño peppers can sting and irritate the skin, so wear rubber gloves when handling peppers and do not touch your eyes.*

**1.** Spray large nonstick saucepan with nonstick cooking spray; heat over medium heat. Cook and stir chicken and onion 5 minutes or until chicken is cooked through. Drain fat.

**2.** Add broth, beans, carrots, bell pepper, tomatoes, jalapeño, if desired, chili powder and red pepper to saucepan. Bring to a boil.

**3.** Reduce heat to low; cover and simmer 15 minutes.

*Makes 5 servings*

Prep and Cook Time: 30 minutes

# Chicken and Black Bean Chili

**1 pound boneless skinless chicken thighs, cut into 1-inch chunks**
**2 teaspoons chili powder**
**2 teaspoons ground cumin**
**¾ teaspoon salt**
**1 green bell pepper, diced**
**1 small onion, chopped**
**3 cloves garlic, minced**
**1 can (about 14 ounces) diced tomatoes**
**1 cup chunky salsa**
**1 can (about 15 ounces) black beans, rinsed and drained**
**Toppings: sour cream, diced fresh tomato, diced ripe avocado, shredded Cheddar cheese, sliced green onions, chopped fresh cilantro and tortilla chips (optional)**

SLOW COOKER DIRECTIONS

**1.** Combine chicken, chili powder, cumin and salt in slow cooker; toss to coat.

**2.** Add bell pepper, onion and garlic; mix well. Stir in tomatoes and salsa. Cover; cook on LOW 5 to 6 hours or on HIGH 2½ to 3 hours or until chicken is tender.

**3.** *Increase heat to HIGH.* Stir in beans. Cover; cook 5 to 10 minutes or until beans are heated through. Ladle into bowls; serve with desired toppings. *Makes 4 servings*

# Black and White Chili

1 pound chicken tenders, cut into
   ¾-inch pieces
1 cup coarsely chopped onion
1 can (about 15 ounces) Great
   Northern beans, rinsed and
   drained
1 can (about 15 ounces) black
   beans, rinsed and drained
1 can (about 14 ounces) Mexican-
   style stewed tomatoes
2 tablespoons Texas-style chili
   powder seasoning mix

**1.** Spray large saucepan with nonstick cooking spray; heat over medium heat. Cook and stir chicken and onion 5 to 8 minutes or until chicken is cooked through.

**2.** Stir beans, tomatoes and seasoning mix into saucepan; bring to a boil.

**3.** Reduce heat to low; simmer, uncovered, 10 minutes.

*Makes 6 servings*

**Serving Suggestion:** For a change of pace, this delicious chili is excellent served over cooked rice or pasta.

Prep and Cook Time: 30 minutes

# Chicken & Orzo Soup

1 boneless skinless chicken
    breast, cut into bite-size
    pieces
2 cups chicken broth
1 cup water
⅔ cup shredded carrot
⅓ cup sliced green onions
¼ cup uncooked orzo pasta
1 teaspoon grated fresh ginger
⅛ teaspoon ground turmeric
2 teaspoons lemon juice
    Black pepper
    Sliced green onions (optional)

**1.** Spray medium saucepan with nonstick cooking spray; heat over medium-high heat. Cook and stir chicken 2 to 3 minutes or until cooked through. Remove from saucepan and set aside.

**2.** Combine broth, water, carrot, green onions, orzo, ginger and turmeric in same saucepan. Bring to a boil. Reduce heat; cover and simmer 8 to 10 minutes or until orzo is tender. Stir in chicken and lemon juice; heat through. Season to taste with pepper.

**3.** Ladle into serving bowls. Sprinkle with additional green onions, if desired.

*Makes 2 servings*

# Chunky Chicken and Vegetable Soup

1 tablespoon canola oil
1 boneless skinless chicken breast, diced
½ cup diced green bell pepper
½ cup thinly sliced celery
2 green onions, sliced
3½ cups chicken broth
1 cup water
½ cup sliced carrots
2 tablespoons whipping cream
¼ teaspoon dried thyme
⅛ teaspoon black pepper
1 tablespoon finely chopped fresh parsley (optional)

**1.** Heat oil in large saucepan over medium heat. Add chicken; cook and stir 4 to 5 minutes or until cooked through. Add bell pepper, celery and green onions. Cook and stir 7 minutes or until vegetables are tender.

**2.** Add broth, water, carrots, cream, thyme and black pepper. Simmer 10 minutes or until carrots are tender.

**3.** Ladle into serving bowls. Sprinkle with parsley, if desired.

*Makes 4 servings*

# Potato Chicken Soup

2½ pounds DOLE® Red Potatoes,
   peeled, cut into 1-inch cubes
½ pound DOLE® Peeled Mini
   Carrots, halved
4 cups reduced-sodium chicken
   broth
½ bay leaf
2 teaspoons olive oil
1 small onion, cut into 1-inch
   cubes
1 teaspoon dried tarragon leaves,
   crushed
¼ teaspoon dried thyme leaves,
   crushed
1½ cups cooked diced chicken
1 to 2 tablespoons minced parsley
⅛ teaspoon salt

• Combine potatoes, carrots,
chicken broth and bay leaf in large pot. Bring to boil; reduce heat and
simmer 15 to 20 minutes.

• Heat oil in nonstick skillet. Add onion; cook 6 to 8 minutes or until
lightly browned. Add tarragon and thyme; cook 30 seconds.

• Add onion mixture, chicken, parsley and salt to soup in pot. Cook
5 minutes longer or until heated through. Remove bay leaf before
serving.                                        *Makes 4 servings*

Prep Time: 25 minutes • Cook Time: 35 minutes

# Chicken Stew

4 to 5 cups chopped cooked
    chicken
1 can (28 ounces) whole
    tomatoes, undrained,
    chopped
2 large potatoes, cut into 1-inch
    pieces
8 ounces fresh okra, sliced
1 large onion, chopped
1 can (14 ounces) cream-style corn
½ cup ketchup
½ cup barbecue sauce

### SLOW COOKER DIRECTIONS

**1.** Combine chicken, tomatoes with juice, potatoes, okra and onion in slow cooker.

**2.** Cover; cook on LOW 6 to 8 hours or until potatoes are tender.

**3.** *Turn heat to HIGH.* Add corn, ketchup and barbecue sauce. Cover; cook on HIGH 30 minutes.

*Makes 6 servings*

**Serving Suggestion:** Serve this stew with hot crusty rolls and a green salad.

# Quick Fix Dishes

## Penne with Roasted Chicken & Vegetables

1 whole roasted chicken (about 2 pounds)
1 package (16 ounces) penne pasta
1 pound roasted vegetables, cut into bite-size pieces
⅓ cup shredded Parmesan cheese
Freshly ground black pepper

**1.** Remove chicken meat from bones and shred. Discard bones and skin.

**2.** Cook pasta according to package directions; drain and return to saucepan.

**3.** Add chicken and vegetables to saucepan; toss until heated through. Sprinkle with cheese and season with pepper.                *Makes 6 servings*

**Tip:** Cook twice as much pasta as you need one night and get a head start on the next pasta meal. Thoroughly drain the pasta you are not using immediately. Plunge it into a bowl of ice water to stop the cooking. Drain completely and toss with olive oil. Cover and refrigerate up to three days. To reheat the pasta, microwave on HIGH 2 to 4 minutes, stirring halfway through.

# Caribbean Chutney Kabobs

**20 (4-inch) wooden skewers\***
**½ medium pineapple**
**¾ pound boneless skinless chicken breasts, cut into 1-inch pieces**
**1 medium red bell pepper, cut into 1-inch pieces**
**½ cup mango chutney**
**2 tablespoons orange juice or pineapple juice**
**1 teaspoon vanilla**
**¼ teaspoon ground nutmeg**

*\*To prevent burning, soak skewers in water at least 20 minutes before assembling kabobs.*

**1.** Peel and core pineapple. Cut pineapple into 1-inch chunks. Alternately thread chicken, pineapple and bell pepper onto skewers. Place in shallow baking dish.

**2.** Combine chutney, orange juice, vanilla and nutmeg in small bowl; mix well. Pour over kabobs. Cover and refrigerate up to 4 hours.

**3.** Preheat broiler. Spray broiler pan with nonstick cooking spray. Place kabobs on prepared broiler pan; discard marinade. Broil kabobs 6 to 8 inches from heat 4 to 5 minutes on each side or until chicken is cooked through. *Makes 10 servings*

# Spicy Chicken Stromboli

1 cup frozen broccoli florets,
  thawed
1 can (10 ounces) chunk white
  chicken packed in water,
  drained
1½ cups (6 ounces) shredded
  Monterey Jack cheese with
  jalapeño peppers
¼ cup chunky salsa
2 green onions, thinly sliced
1 package (10 ounces)
  refrigerated pizza dough

**1.** Preheat oven to 400°F. Coarsely chop broccoli. Combine broccoli, chicken, cheese, salsa and green onions in medium bowl.

**2.** Unroll pizza dough. Pat into 15×10-inch rectangle. Sprinkle broccoli mixture evenly over top. Starting with long side, tightly roll up jelly-roll style. Pinch seam to seal. Place on baking sheet, seam side down.

**3.** Bake 15 to 20 minutes or until golden brown. Transfer to wire rack to cool slightly. Slice and serve warm. *Makes 6 servings*

**Serving Suggestion:** Serve with salsa on the side for dipping or pour salsa on top of slices for a boost of added flavor.

Prep and Cook Time: 30 minutes

# Pesto-Coated Baked Chicken

**1 pound boneless skinless chicken breasts**
**¼ cup plus 1 tablespoon prepared pesto**
**1½ teaspoons sour cream**
**1½ teaspoons mayonnaise**
**1 tablespoon shredded Parmesan cheese**
**1 tablespoon pine nuts**

**1.** Preheat oven to 450°F. Arrange chicken in single layer in shallow baking pan.

**2.** Combine pesto, sour cream and mayonnaise in small cup. Brush over chicken. Sprinkle with cheese and pine nuts.

**3.** Bake 8 to 10 minutes or until chicken is no longer pink in center.

*Makes 4 servings*

# Chicken and Vegetable Pasta

**8 ounces uncooked bowtie pasta**
**3 boneless skinless chicken breasts**
**2 red or green bell peppers, cut into quarters**
**1 medium zucchini, cut in half lengthwise**
**½ cup Italian dressing**
**½ cup prepared pesto**

**1.** Cook pasta according to package directions. Drain. Transfer to large bowl; keep warm. Combine chicken, bell peppers, zucchini and dressing in medium bowl; toss well.

**2.** Prepare grill for direct cooking or preheat broiler.

**3.** Grill or broil chicken and vegetables 6 to 8 minutes on each side or until chicken is no longer pink in center. Cut chicken and vegetables into bite-size pieces. Add chicken, vegetables and pesto to pasta; toss well.

*Makes 4 to 6 servings*

Prep and Cook Time: 20 minutes

# Chicken & Mushrooms with Pasta & Roasted Garlic Sauce

**8 ounces rotini or fusilli pasta**
**1 teaspoon olive oil**
**4 boneless skinless chicken breasts**
**1 jar (about 28 ounces) roasted garlic pasta sauce**
**1 cup sliced mushrooms**
   **Grated Parmesan cheese (optional)**

**1.** Cook pasta according to package directions. Drain. Set aside; keep warm.

**2.** Heat oil in large skillet over medium heat. Lightly brown chicken 1 to 2 minutes per side. Remove from skillet; cut into thin strips. Return to skillet.

**3.** Stir in pasta sauce and mushrooms. Cover and simmer 10 minutes or until chicken is cooked through. Stir in pasta. Sprinkle with cheese, if desired. *Makes 4 servings*

**Tip:** Chicken breasts, the white meat of the chicken, are a popular cut, but they are also the most expensive. To save money and for a richer tasting dish, choose chicken thighs, the dark meat. Thighs are also available boneless and skinless for easier preparation. Chicken breasts may be substituted with thighs in most recipes.

# Chicken Breasts Smothered in Tomatoes and Mozzarella

**4 boneless skinless chicken breasts**
**3 tablespoons olive oil, divided**
**1 cup chopped onion**
**2 teaspoons minced garlic**
**1 can (about 14 ounces) Italian-style stewed tomatoes**
**1½ cups (6 ounces) shredded mozzarella cheese**

**1.** Preheat broiler. Pound chicken breasts between 2 pieces of plastic wrap to ¼-inch thickness using flat side of meat mallet or rolling pin. Heat 2 tablespoons oil in ovenproof skillet over medium heat. Add chicken; cook 3 to 4 minutes per side or until no longer pink in center. Transfer to plate; cover and keep warm.

**2.** Heat remaining 1 tablespoon oil in same skillet over medium heat. Add onion and garlic; cook and stir 3 minutes. Add tomatoes; bring to a simmer. Return chicken to skillet; spoon onion and tomato mixture over chicken.

**3.** Sprinkle cheese over top. Broil 4 to 5 inches from heat or until cheese is melted. *Makes 4 servings*

Prep and Cook Time: 20 minutes

# Saucy Tomato Chicken

8 ounces uncooked egg noodles
1 can (about 14 ounces) stewed tomatoes with onions, celery and
   green bell pepper
2 cloves garlic, minced
1 teaspoon dried oregano
4 boneless skinless chicken breasts
2 teaspoons olive oil

**1.** Cook noodles according to package directions; drain. Meanwhile, place tomatoes, garlic and oregano in large nonstick skillet. Bring to a boil over high heat; boil, stirring constantly, 5 minutes or until liquid is reduced and tomato mixture becomes slightly darker in color. (Mixture will be thick.) Transfer to small bowl; keep warm. Wipe out skillet.

**2.** Spray same skillet with nonstick cooking spray. Cook chicken over medium-high heat 6 minutes. Turn; reduce heat to medium-low. Spoon tomato mixture into skillet around chicken. Cover; cook 4 minutes or until chicken is no longer pink in center.

**3.** Place noodles on serving platter; top with chicken. Add oil to tomato mixture; blend well. Spoon tomato mixture evenly over chicken.

*Makes 4 servings*

# Sandwiches & Salads

## Stir-Fry Pita Sandwiches

- **12 ounces chicken tenders**
- **1 onion, thinly sliced**
- **1 red bell pepper, cut into strips**
- **½ cup zesty Italian dressing**
- **¼ teaspoon red pepper flakes**
- **4 pita bread rounds**
- **8 leaves leaf lettuce**
- **¼ cup crumbled feta cheese**

**1.** Cut chicken tenders into quarters. Coat large nonstick skillet with nonstick cooking spray. Cook and stir chicken over medium heat 3 minutes. Add onion and bell pepper; cook and stir 2 minutes. Add Italian dressing and red pepper flakes; cover and cook 3 minutes or until chicken is cooked through. Remove from heat; uncover and let cool 5 minutes.

**2.** Meanwhile, cut pita bread rounds in half to form pockets. Line each pocket with lettuce leaf.

**3.** Spoon chicken filling into pockets; sprinkle with feta cheese.

*Makes 4 servings*

**Tip:** Salad dressings offer a surprising amount of convenience in the kitchen. Their basic components of oil, vinegar, herbs and spices provide a ready-made marinade or seasoned oil for cooking meats and poultry.

Prep and Cook Time: 17 minutes

# Sunburst Chicken Salad

1 tablespoon mayonnaise
1 tablespoon sour cream
2 teaspoons frozen orange juice concentrate, thawed
¼ teaspoon grated orange peel
2 boneless skinless chicken breasts, cooked and chopped
1 large kiwi, thinly sliced
⅓ cup canned mandarin oranges, drained
¼ cup finely chopped celery
4 lettuce leaves
2 tablespoons coarsely chopped cashews

**1.** Combine mayonnaise, sour cream, orange juice concentrate and orange peel in medium bowl.

**2.** Add chicken, kiwi, oranges and celery; toss to coat. Cover and refrigerate 2 hours.

**3.** Serve on lettuce leaves. Sprinkle with cashews.     *Makes 2 servings*

# Asian Wraps

8 ounces boneless skinless
   chicken breasts or thighs, cut
   into ½-inch pieces
1 teaspoon minced fresh ginger
1 teaspoon minced garlic
¼ teaspoon red pepper flakes
¼ cup reduced-sodium teriyaki
   sauce
4 cups (about 8 ounces) packaged
   coleslaw mix
½ cup sliced green onions
4 (10-inch) flour tortillas
8 teaspoons plum fruit spread

**1.** Spray nonstick wok or large skillet with nonstick cooking spray; heat over medium-high heat. Stir-fry chicken 2 minutes. Add ginger, garlic and pepper flakes; stir-fry 2 minutes.

**2.** Add teriyaki sauce; mix well.\* Add coleslaw mix and green onions; stir-fry 4 minutes or until chicken is cooked through and cabbage is crisp-tender.

**3.** Spread each tortilla with 2 teaspoons fruit spread; evenly spoon chicken mixture down center of tortillas. Roll up to form wraps.

*Makes 4 servings*

\**If sauce is too thick, add up to 2 tablespoons water to thin it.*

Prep Time: 10 minutes • Cook Time: 10 minutes

# Garden Pasta Salad

6 cups (about 12 ounces) cooked penne pasta
2 cups shredded cooked boneless skinless chicken breasts
¾ cup chopped red onion
¾ cup diced red or green bell pepper
¾ cup sliced zucchini
1 can (4 ounces) sliced black olives, drained
1 teaspoon red pepper flakes
1 teaspoon salt
1 can (10¾ ounces) condensed cream of chicken soup, undiluted
½ cup lemon juice
½ cup grated Parmesan cheese
½ cup chopped fresh basil (optional)
¼ cup chopped fresh parsley (optional)

**1.** Combine pasta, chicken, onion, bell pepper, zucchini, olives, red pepper flakes and salt in large bowl; toss lightly.

**2.** Combine soup and lemon juice in small bowl. Pour soup mixture over pasta salad; toss to combine.

**3.** Sprinkle with Parmesan cheese, basil and parsley, if desired.

*Makes 8 servings*

# Blackened Chicken Salad in Pitas

- **1 tablespoon paprika**
- **1 teaspoon onion powder**
- **½ teaspoon garlic powder**
- **½ teaspoon dried oregano**
- **½ teaspoon dried thyme**
- **¼ teaspoon salt**
- **¼ teaspoon white pepper**
- **¼ teaspoon ground red pepper**
- **¼ teaspoon black pepper**
- **2 boneless skinless chicken breasts**
- **4 pita bread rounds**
- **1 cup chopped spinach leaves**
- **2 small tomatoes, cut into 8 slices**
- **8 thin slices cucumber**
- **½ cup prepared ranch dressing**

**1.** Spray cold grid with nonstick cooking spray. Prepare grill for direct cooking. Combine paprika, onion powder, garlic powder, oregano, thyme, salt, white pepper, red pepper and black pepper in small bowl. Rub on all surfaces of chicken. Grill chicken on covered grill over medium-hot coals 10 minutes per side or until chicken is no longer pink in center. Cool slightly. Cut into thin strips.

**2.** Wrap 2 pita bread rounds in paper towels. Microwave on HIGH 20 to 30 seconds or just until warm. Repeat with remaining pita bread rounds. Cut in half to form pockets.

**3.** Divide chicken strips, spinach, tomato slices, cucumber slices and ranch dressing among pita bread halves. Serve warm.

*Makes 4 servings*

# Chicken and Mozzarella Melts

2 cloves garlic, crushed
4 boneless skinless chicken breasts
⅛ teaspoon salt
⅛ teaspoon black pepper
1 tablespoon prepared pesto
4 small hard rolls, split
12 fresh spinach leaves
8 fresh basil leaves* (optional)
3 plum tomatoes, sliced
½ cup (2 ounces) shredded mozzarella cheese

*Omit basil leaves if fresh are unavailable. Do not substitute dried basil.*

**1.** Preheat oven to 350°F. Rub garlic on all surfaces of chicken. Spray medium nonstick skillet with nonstick cooking spray; heat over medium heat. Cook chicken 5 to 6 minutes on each side or until no longer pink in center. Sprinkle with salt and pepper.

**2.** Brush pesto onto bottom halves of rolls; layer with spinach, basil, if desired, and tomatoes. Place chicken in rolls; sprinkle cheese evenly over chicken. (If desired, sandwiches may be prepared up to this point and wrapped in foil. Refrigerate until ready to bake. Bake in preheated 350°F oven until chicken is warmed through, about 20 minutes.)

**3.** Wrap sandwiches in foil; bake about 10 minutes or until cheese is melted.                                    *Makes 4 servings*

# Easy Thai Chicken Sandwiches

¼ cup peanut butter
2 tablespoons honey
2 tablespoons reduced-sodium
soy sauce
½ teaspoon garlic powder
½ teaspoon ground ginger
4 boneless skinless chicken
breasts
4 onion or kaiser rolls, split
Lettuce leaves
1 cup sliced cucumber
1 cup bean sprouts
¼ cup sliced green onions

**1.** Preheat oven to 400°F. Combine peanut butter, honey, soy sauce, garlic powder and ginger in large bowl; stir until well blended. Reserve ¼ cup peanut butter mixture.

**2.** Place chicken on foil-lined baking pan. Spread remaining peanut butter mixture over chicken. Bake 20 minutes or until chicken is no longer pink in center.

**3.** Fill rolls with lettuce, cucumber, bean sprouts and chicken; sprinkle with green onions. Serve with reserved peanut butter mixture.

*Makes 4 servings*

# Chicken and Spinach Salad

¾ **pound chicken tenders**
4 **cups shredded stemmed spinach**
2 **cups torn romaine lettuce**
1 **large grapefruit, peeled and sectioned**
8 **thin slices red onion, separated into rings**
2 **tablespoons crumbled blue cheese**
½ **cup frozen citrus blend concentrate, thawed**
¼ **cup prepared Italian salad dressing**

**1.** Cut chicken into 2×½-inch strips. Spray large nonstick skillet with nonstick cooking spray; heat over medium heat. Cook and stir chicken 5 minutes or until cooked through.

**2.** Divide spinach, lettuce, grapefruit, onion, cheese and chicken among 4 salad plates.

**3.** Combine citrus blend concentrate and Italian dressing in small bowl; drizzle over salads. *Makes 4 servings*

# Chicken and Pear Pita Pockets

**3 cups diced cooked chicken**
**1 can (15 ounces) Bartlett Pear**
**halves or slices, thoroughly**
**drained and diced**
**¾ cup chopped celery**
**½ cup raisins or chopped dates**
**¼ cup each nonfat plain yogurt**
**and lowfat mayonnaise**
**1 teaspoon each salt, lemon**
**pepper and dried rosemary**
**leaves, crushed**
**6 pita pocket breads, halved**
**12 lettuce leaves**

Combine chicken, pears, celery and raisins in medium bowl. Prepare dressing by blending yogurt, mayonnaise, salt, lemon pepper and rosemary. Combine dressing and pear mixture; mix well. Refrigerate until serving. To serve, line each pita half with lettuce leaf. Portion ½ cup mixture into each half.

*Makes 6 servings*

Favorite recipe from **Pacific Northwest Canned Pear Service**

# Mustard-Glazed Chicken Sandwiches

½ **cup honey-mustard barbecue sauce, divided**
4 **kaiser rolls, split**
4 **boneless skinless chicken breasts**
4 **slices Swiss cheese**
4 **leaves leaf lettuce**
8 **slices tomato**

**1.** Spread about 1 teaspoon barbecue sauce on cut sides of each roll. Pound chicken breasts between 2 pieces of plastic wrap to ½-inch thickness with flat side of meat mallet or rolling pin. Spread remaining barbecue sauce over chicken.

**2.** Spray large nonstick skillet with nonstick cooking spray; heat over medium heat. Cook chicken 5 minutes per side or until no longer pink in center. Remove from heat. Top chicken with cheese; let stand 3 minutes to melt.

**3.** Place lettuce leaves and tomato slices on bottom halves of rolls; top with chicken and top halves of rolls. *Makes 4 servings*

**Serving Suggestion:** Serve sandwiches with yellow tomatoes, baby carrots and celery sticks.

Prep and Cook Time: 19 minutes

# Basil Chicken and Vegetables on Focaccia

½ cup mayonnaise
½ teaspoon black pepper, divided
¼ teaspoon garlic powder
1 loaf (16 ounces) focaccia or Italian bread
4 boneless skinless chicken breasts
3 tablespoons olive oil
2 cloves garlic, minced
1½ teaspoons dried basil
½ teaspoon salt
1 green bell pepper, cut into quarters
1 medium zucchini, cut lengthwise into 4 slices
2 plum tomatoes, sliced

**1.** Combine mayonnaise, ¼ teaspoon black pepper and garlic powder in small bowl; set aside. Cut focaccia into quarters. Cut each quarter horizontally in half; set aside.

**2.** Spray cold grid with nonstick cooking spray. Prepare grill for direct cooking. Combine chicken, oil, garlic, basil, salt and remaining ¼ teaspoon black pepper in large resealable food storage bag. Seal bag; knead to combine. Add bell pepper and zucchini; knead to coat.

**3.** Grill chicken, bell pepper and zucchini over medium heat 6 to 8 minutes on each side or until chicken is no longer pink in center. (Bell pepper and zucchini may take less time.) Top bottom halves of focaccia with mayonnaise mixture, tomatoes, bell pepper, zucchini and chicken. Top with top halves of focaccia.          *Makes 4 servings*

# Cobb Salad

1 package (10 ounces) torn mixed
   salad greens *or* 8 cups torn
   romaine lettuce
6 ounces deli chicken, cut ¼ inch
   thick
1 large tomato, seeded and
   chopped
⅓ cup bacon bits or crumbled
   crisp-cooked bacon
1 large ripe avocado, diced
⅓ cup prepared blue cheese or
   Caesar salad dressing

**1.** Place lettuce in salad bowl. Dice chicken; place in center of lettuce.

**2.** Arrange tomato, bacon and avocado in rows on either side of chicken.

**3.** Drizzle with dressing. Serve immediately.          *Makes 4 servings*

**Serving Suggestion:** Serve with warm French or Italian rolls.

# Apricot Chicken Sandwiches

**6 ounces chicken tenders, cooked and diced**
**2 tablespoons chopped fresh apricots**
**2 tablespoons apricot fruit spread**
**4 slices whole wheat bread**
**4 lettuce leaves**

**1.** Combine chicken, apricots and fruit spread in medium bowl.

**2.** Top 2 bread slices with lettuce. Top evenly with chicken mixture and top with remaining 2 bread slices. Cut sandwiches into quarters.

*Makes 4 servings*

**Tip:** Domestically grown apricots are available from late May to early August. Imports are found sporadically throughout the rest of the year. Ripe apricots are very fragile; consequently, they must be picked when hard and shipped under refrigeration. Ripen apricots by placing them in a paper bag at room temperature for up to three or four days. Store ripe apricots in a plastic bag in the refrigerator for a day or two at most.

# Monterey Chicken Sandwiches

- **1 tablespoon vegetable oil**
- **1 tablespoon butter**
- **4 boneless skinless chicken breasts**
- **1 teaspoon dried thyme**
- **½ teaspoon salt**
- **¼ teaspoon black pepper**
- **1 large red onion, thinly sliced**
- **4 kaiser rolls, split**
- **Radicchio or lettuce leaves**

**1.** Heat oil and butter in large skillet over medium heat. Add chicken; sprinkle with thyme. Cook 8 minutes or until browned on both sides and no longer pink in center, turning after 4 minutes. Season with salt and pepper. Remove from skillet; keep warm.

**2.** Cook and stir onion in same skillet until translucent.

**3.** Fill rolls with radicchio leaves, chicken and onion.

*Makes 4 sandwiches*

**Serving Suggestion:** Serve with mango chutney, olives and corn on the cob.

# Sizzling Stir-Fry

## Pineapple Basil Chicken Supreme

1 can (8 ounces) pineapple chunks in unsweetened juice
2 teaspoons cornstarch
2 tablespoons peanut oil
1 pound boneless skinless chicken breasts, cut into ¾-inch pieces
2 to 4 serrano peppers,* cut into thin strips (optional)
2 cloves garlic, minced
2 green onions, cut into 1-inch pieces
¾ cup roasted unsalted cashews
¼ cup chopped fresh basil (do not use dried)
1 tablespoon fish sauce**
1 tablespoon soy sauce
Hot cooked rice

*Serrano peppers can sting and irritate the skin, so wear rubber gloves when handling peppers and do not touch your eyes.

**Fish sauce is available at most large supermarkets and Asian markets.

**1.** Drain pineapple, reserving juice. Combine reserved juice and cornstarch in small bowl; set aside.

**2.** Heat wok or large skillet over high heat 1 minute. Drizzle oil into wok; heat 30 seconds. Add chicken, serrano peppers, if desired, and garlic; stir-fry 3 minutes or until chicken is cooked through. Add green onions; stir-fry 1 minute.

**3.** Stir cornstarch mixture; add to wok. Cook and stir 1 minute or until thickened. Add pineapple, cashews, basil, fish sauce and soy sauce; cook and stir 1 minute or until heated through. Serve over rice.

*Makes 4 servings*

# Golden Chicken Stir-Fry

½ **pound chicken tenders, cut into thin strips**
½ **cup stir-fry sauce, divided**
3 **tablespoons vegetable oil, divided**
1 **medium onion, thinly sliced**
2 **carrots, cut diagonally into thin slices**
1 **stalk celery, cut diagonally into thin slices**
1 **clove garlic, minced**
1 **tablespoon sesame seeds, toasted***
½ **teaspoon Chinese five-spice powder**
¼ **teaspoon dark sesame oil**
2 **cups hot cooked rice**

*To toast sesame seeds, spread seeds in small skillet. Shake skillet over medium-low heat 3 minutes or until seeds begin to pop and turn golden.*

**1.** Toss chicken with 2 tablespoons stir-fry sauce in small bowl. Heat 1 tablespoon vegetable oil in large skillet or wok over medium-high heat. Add chicken; stir-fry 2 to 3 minutes or until cooked through; remove from skillet.

**2.** Heat remaining 2 tablespoons vegetable oil in same skillet. Add onion; stir-fry 2 minutes. Add carrots, celery and garlic; stir-fry 2 minutes.

**3.** Add remaining ¼ cup plus 2 tablespoons stir-fry sauce, chicken mixture, sesame seeds and five-spice powder to skillet. Cook and stir until chicken and vegetables are coated with sauce. Remove from heat; stir in sesame oil. Serve with rice. *Makes 4 servings*

# Sesame Chicken

1 pound boneless skinless chicken
    breasts or thighs
⅔ cup teriyaki sauce, divided
2 teaspoons cornstarch
1 tablespoon peanut or
    vegetable oil
2 cloves garlic, minced
2 green onions, cut into ½-inch
    slices
1 tablespoon sesame seeds,
    toasted*
1 teaspoon dark sesame oil

*To toast sesame seeds, spread seeds in small skillet. Shake skillet over medium-low heat 3 minutes or until seeds begin to pop and turn golden.

**1.** Cut chicken into 1-inch pieces; toss with ⅓ cup teriyaki sauce in medium bowl. Marinate in refrigerator 15 to 20 minutes.

**2.** Drain chicken; discard marinade. Combine remaining ⅓ cup teriyaki sauce and cornstarch in small bowl; stir until smooth.

**3.** Heat peanut oil in wok or large skillet over medium-high heat. Add chicken and garlic; stir-fry 3 minutes or until chicken is cooked through. Stir cornstarch mixture; add to wok. Cook and stir 1 minute or until sauce boils and thickens. Stir in green onions, sesame seeds and sesame oil. Serve immediately. *Makes 4 servings*

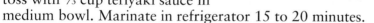

# Thai Curry Stir-Fry

½ cup chicken broth
2 teaspoons cornstarch
2 teaspoons reduced-sodium soy sauce
1½ teaspoons curry powder
⅛ teaspoon red pepper flakes
3 teaspoons peanut oil, divided
3 green onions, sliced
2 cloves garlic, minced
2 cups broccoli florets
⅔ cup sliced carrots
8 ounces boneless skinless chicken breasts, cut into bite-size pieces
1 cup hot cooked rice

**1.** Combine broth, cornstarch, soy sauce, curry powder and red pepper flakes in small bowl; mix well. Set aside.

**2.** Heat 2 teaspoons oil in wok or large nonstick skillet over medium-high heat. Stir-fry green onions and garlic 1 minute. Remove from wok. Stir-fry broccoli and carrots 2 to 3 minutes or until crisp-tender. Remove from wok.

**3.** Heat remaining 1 teaspoon oil in wok. Add chicken; stir-fry 2 to 3 minutes or until cooked through. Stir cornstarch mixture; add to wok. Cook and stir until sauce comes to a boil and thickens slightly. Return all vegetables to wok; cook and stir until heated through. Serve over rice.

*Makes 2 servings*

# Shanghai Chicken with Asparagus and Ham

2 cups diagonally cut 1-inch
    asparagus pieces*
2 teaspoons vegetable oil
¾ cup coarsely chopped onion
2 cloves garlic, minced
1 pound boneless skinless chicken
    breasts, cut into 1-inch pieces
2 tablespoons teriyaki sauce
¼ cup diced deli ham
2 cups hot cooked vermicelli
    noodles

*Or substitute thawed frozen asparagus;
omit step 1.

**1.** To blanch asparagus pieces, cook 3 minutes in enough boiling water to cover. Plunge asparagus into cold water. Drain well.

**2.** Heat oil in large nonstick skillet over medium heat. Add onion and garlic; stir-fry 2 minutes. Add chicken; stir-fry 2 minutes. Add asparagus; stir-fry 2 minutes or until chicken is cooked through.

**3.** Add teriyaki sauce; mix well. Add ham; stir-fry until heated through. Serve over noodles. *Makes 4 servings*

# Chicken and Asparagus Stir-Fry

1 cup uncooked rice
2 tablespoons vegetable oil
1 pound boneless skinless chicken
    breasts, cut into ½-inch-wide
    strips
2 medium red bell peppers, cut
    into thin strips
½ pound fresh asparagus,* cut
    diagonally into 1-inch pieces
½ cup stir-fry sauce

*For stir-frying, select thin stalks of
asparagus.

**1.** Cook rice according to package directions; keep warm.

**2.** Heat oil in wok or large skillet over medium-high heat. Stir-fry chicken 3 to 4 minutes or until cooked through.

**3.** Stir in bell peppers and asparagus; reduce heat to medium. Cover; cook 2 minutes or until vegetables are crisp-tender, stirring occasionally. Stir in sauce; heat through. Serve with rice. *Makes 4 servings*

# Easy Make-at-Home Chinese Chicken

3 tablespoons frozen orange juice concentrate, thawed
2 tablespoons water
2 tablespoons reduced-sodium soy sauce
¾ teaspoon cornstarch
¼ teaspoon garlic powder
2 carrots, sliced
1 package (12 ounces) frozen broccoli and cauliflower florets, thawed
2 teaspoons canola oil
¾ pound boneless skinless chicken breasts, cut into bite-size pieces
1⅓ cups hot cooked rice

**1.** Combine orange juice concentrate, water, soy sauce, cornstarch and garlic powder in small bowl; set aside.

**2.** Spray nonstick wok or large skillet with nonstick cooking spray; heat over high heat. Stir-fry carrots 1 minute. Add broccoli and cauliflower; stir-fry 2 to 3 minutes or until vegetables are crisp-tender. Remove vegetables from wok.

**3.** Heat oil in wok over medium-high heat. Stir-fry chicken 2 to 3 minutes or until cooked through. Push chicken up side of wok. Stir sauce; add to wok. Bring to a boil. Return vegetables to wok; cook and stir until heated through. Serve over rice. *Makes 4 servings*

**Tip:** To cut carrots decoratively, use a citrus stripper or grapefruit spoon to cut 4 or 5 grooves into whole carrots, cutting lengthwise from stem end to tip. Then cut carrots crosswise into slices.

# Sausage and Chicken Jambalaya Stir-Fry

   1 cup uncooked rice
   1 teaspoon vegetable oil
   ¼ pound chicken tenders, cut into 1-inch pieces
   ½ pound smoked Polish sausage, cut into bite-size pieces
   1 large onion, chopped
   ¾ cup diced green bell pepper
   1 teaspoon minced garlic
   1 can (about 14 ounces) diced tomatoes
   ½ cup chicken broth
   1 tablespoon dried parsley
   ½ teaspoon dried thyme
   ¼ teaspoon salt
   ¼ teaspoon black pepper
   ⅛ to ¼ teaspoon ground red pepper

**1.** Cook rice according to package directions. Meanwhile, heat oil in wok or large skillet over medium-high heat. Stir-fry chicken 2 minutes. Add sausage; stir-fry 4 minutes or until sausage and chicken are cooked through. Remove from wok to medium bowl.

**2.** Place onion and bell pepper in wok; reduce heat to low. Cover and cook 2 to 3 minutes, stirring once or twice. Stir in garlic; cook, uncovered, 1 minute.

**3.** Add sausage, chicken, tomatoes, broth, parsley, thyme, salt, black pepper and red pepper. Bring to a boil. Reduce heat to medium-low; simmer, uncovered, 5 minutes or until most liquid has evaporated. Stir in rice; heat through.                    *Makes 4 servings*

Prep and Cook Time: 30 minutes

# Mandarin Orange Chicken

2 tablespoons rice vinegar
2 tablespoons olive oil, divided
2 tablespoons soy sauce
2 teaspoons grated orange peel
1 clove garlic, minced
1 pound boneless skinless chicken breasts, cut into strips
2 cans (11 ounces each) mandarin oranges, undrained
½ cup orange juice
2 tablespoons cornstarch
½ teaspoon red pepper flakes
1 onion, cut into thin wedges
1 small zucchini, sliced
1 red bell pepper, cut into 1-inch pieces
   Hot cooked rice

**1.** Combine vinegar, 1 tablespoon oil, soy sauce, orange peel and garlic in medium bowl. Add chicken; toss to coat. Cover and refrigerate 15 minutes to 1 hour.

**2.** Drain chicken, reserving marinade. Drain oranges into 2-cup measuring cup; set oranges aside. Add marinade to cup, plus additional orange juice if needed to make 2 cups liquid. Whisk orange juice mixture into cornstarch and red pepper flakes in medium bowl; set aside.

**3.** Heat remaining 1 tablespoon oil in wok or large skillet over high heat. Add chicken; stir-fry 2 to 3 minutes or until cooked through. Remove chicken. Stir-fry onion 1 minute. Add zucchini; stir-fry 1 minute. Add bell pepper; stir-fry 1 minute or until all vegetables are crisp-tender. Stir orange juice mixture; add to wok. Cook and stir until mixture comes to a boil; boil 1 minute. Add chicken; heat through. Gently stir in oranges. Serve with rice. *Makes 6 servings*

# Orzo with Chicken and Cabbage

 8 ounces uncooked orzo pasta
¼ cup rice vinegar
¼ cup chicken broth
 2 tablespoons brown sugar
 2 tablespoons soy sauce
 1 teaspoon cornstarch
 1 tablespoon sesame chili oil
 2 cups thinly sliced red cabbage
 1 tablespoon seasoned stir-fry or
    hot oil
 1 pound boneless skinless chicken
    breasts or tenders, cut into
    bite-size pieces
 4 ounces snow peas
 4 green onions (separating white
    and green parts), sliced into
    ½-inch pieces
 1 tablespoon sesame seeds, toasted*

*To toast sesame seeds, spread seeds in small skillet. Shake skillet over medium-low heat 3 minutes or until seeds begin to pop and turn golden.*

**1.** Cook orzo according to package directions until al dente. Drain. Set aside; keep warm. Whisk together vinegar, broth, brown sugar, soy sauce and cornstarch in small bowl; set aside.

**2.** Heat sesame chili oil in wok or large skillet over high heat. Add cabbage; stir-fry 2 to 3 minutes or until crisp-tender. Remove from wok; keep warm.

**3.** Heat stir-fry oil in wok over high heat. Add chicken; stir-fry 3 minutes or until cooked through. Add snow peas and white parts of green onions; stir-fry 1 to 2 minutes or until vegetables are crisp-tender. Stir vinegar mixture; add to wok, stirring until hot and slightly thickened. Add orzo and cabbage; toss to combine. Sprinkle with green onion tops and sesame seeds.           *Makes 4 servings*

# Chicken and Vegetables with Mustard Sauce

1 tablespoon sugar
2 teaspoons cornstarch
1½ teaspoons dry mustard
2 tablespoons water
2 tablespoons rice vinegar
2 tablespoons reduced-sodium
    soy sauce
1 pound boneless skinless chicken
    breasts
4 teaspoons vegetable oil,
    divided
2 cloves garlic, minced
1 small red bell pepper, cut into
    short thin strips
½ cup thinly sliced celery
1 small onion, cut into thin
    wedges
3 cups hot cooked Chinese egg noodles (3 ounces uncooked)

**1.** Combine sugar, cornstarch and dry mustard in small bowl. Stir in water, vinegar and soy sauce until smooth. Cut chicken into 1-inch pieces.

**2.** Heat 2 teaspoons oil in wok or large nonstick skillet over medium heat. Add chicken and garlic; stir-fry 3 minutes or until chicken is cooked though. Remove from wok.

**3.** Heat remaining 2 teaspoons oil in wok. Add bell pepper, celery and onion; stir-fry 3 minutes or until vegetables are crisp-tender. Stir soy sauce mixture; add to wok. Cook and stir 30 seconds or until sauce boils and thickens. Return chicken with any accumulated juices to wok; heat through. Serve over Chinese noodles. *Makes 4 servings*

# Chicken Chow Mein

1 pound boneless skinless chicken breasts, cut into thin strips
2 cloves garlic, minced
2 tablespoons vegetable oil, divided
2 tablespoons dry sherry
2 tablespoons reduced-sodium soy sauce
2 cups (about 7 ounces) fresh snow peas, cut into halves *or* 1 package
(7 ounces) frozen snow peas, thawed
3 green onions, cut diagonally into 1-inch pieces
1½ cups Chinese egg noodles or vermicelli, cooked and drained
(4 ounces uncooked)
1 teaspoon dark sesame oil (optional)
Chopped red bell pepper (optional)

**1.** Combine chicken and garlic in medium bowl. Heat 1 tablespoon vegetable oil in wok or large nonstick skillet over medium-high heat. Add chicken mixture; stir-fry 3 minutes or until chicken is cooked through. Transfer to medium bowl; toss with sherry and soy sauce.

**2.** Heat remaining 1 tablespoon vegetable oil in wok. Add snow peas; stir-fry 2 minutes for fresh or 1 minute for frozen snow peas. Add green onions; stir-fry 30 seconds. Add chicken mixture; stir-fry 1 minute.

**3.** Add noodles to wok; stir-fry 2 minutes or until heated through. Stir in sesame oil, if desired; garnish with bell pepper.          *Makes 4 servings*

# *Comforting Casseroles*

## Heartland Chicken Casserole

    10 slices white bread, cubed
 1½ cups cracker crumbs or dry bread crumbs, divided
     4 cups cubed cooked chicken
     3 cups chicken broth
     1 cup chopped onion
     1 cup chopped celery
     1 can (8 ounces) sliced mushrooms, drained
     1 jar (about 4 ounces) pimientos, diced
     3 eggs, lightly beaten
        Salt and black pepper
     1 tablespoon butter

**1.** Preheat oven to 350°F. Combine bread cubes and 1 cup cracker crumbs in large bowl. Add chicken, broth, onion, celery, mushrooms, pimientos and eggs; mix well. Season with salt and pepper; spoon into 2½-quart casserole.

**2.** Melt butter in small saucepan. Add remaining ½ cup cracker crumbs; cook and stir until light brown. Sprinkle crumbs over casserole.

**3.** Bake 1 hour or until hot and bubbly.              *Makes 6 servings*

# Chicken, Asparagus & Mushroom Bake

1 tablespoon butter
1 tablespoon olive oil
2 boneless skinless chicken breasts, cut into bite-size pieces
2 cloves garlic, minced
1 cup sliced mushrooms
2 cups sliced asparagus
  Black pepper
1 package (about 6 ounces) corn bread stuffing mix
¼ cup dry white wine (optional)
2 cups reduced-sodium chicken broth
1 can (10¾ ounces) condensed cream of asparagus or cream of chicken
  soup, undiluted

**1.** Preheat oven to 350°F. Heat butter and oil in large skillet over medium-high heat until butter is melted. Add chicken and garlic; cook and stir about 3 minutes or until chicken is cooked through. Add mushrooms; cook and stir 2 minutes. Add asparagus; cook and stir about 5 minutes or until asparagus is crisp-tender. Season with pepper. Transfer mixture to 2½-quart casserole or 6 small casseroles. Top with stuffing mix.

**2.** Add wine to skillet, if desired; cook and stir 1 minute over medium-high heat, scraping up any browned bits from bottom of skillet. Add broth and soup; cook and stir until well blended.

**3.** Pour broth mixture over stuffing mix; mix well. Bake, uncovered, about 35 minutes (30 minutes for small casseroles) or until heated through and lightly browned.                    *Makes 6 servings*

# Cheesy Chicken Enchiladas

¼ cup (½ stick) butter
1 cup chopped onion
2 cloves garlic, minced
¼ cup all-purpose flour
1 cup chicken broth
4 ounces cream cheese, softened and cut into pieces
2 cups (8 ounces) shredded Mexican cheese blend, divided
1 cup shredded cooked chicken
1 can (7 ounces) diced mild green chiles, drained
½ cup diced pimientos
6 (8-inch) flour tortillas, warmed
¼ cup chopped fresh cilantro
¾ cup salsa

**1.** Preheat oven to 350°F. Spray 13×9-inch baking dish with nonstick cooking spray.

**2.** Melt butter in medium saucepan over medium heat. Add onion and garlic; cook and stir until onion is translucent. Add flour; cook and stir 1 minute. Gradually add broth; cook and stir 2 to 3 minutes or until slightly thickened. Add cream cheese; stir until melted. Stir in ½ cup shredded cheese, chicken, chiles and pimientos.

**3.** Spoon about ⅓ cup mixture onto each tortilla. Roll up and place seam side down in prepared dish. Pour remaining mixture over enchiladas; sprinkle with remaining 1½ cups shredded cheese. Bake 20 minutes or until bubbly and lightly browned. Sprinkle with cilantro and serve with salsa. *Makes 6 servings*

# Apple Curry Chicken

4 boneless skinless chicken
  breasts
1 cup apple juice, divided
¼ teaspoon salt
  Dash black pepper
1½ cups plain croutons
1 medium apple, chopped
1 medium onion, chopped
¼ cup raisins
2 teaspoons brown sugar
1 teaspoon curry powder
¾ teaspoon poultry seasoning
⅛ teaspoon garlic powder

**1.** Preheat oven to 350°F. Lightly grease 2-quart baking dish. Arrange chicken breasts in single layer in prepared dish. Combine ¼ cup apple juice, salt and pepper in small bowl. Brush juice mixture over chicken.

**2.** Combine croutons, apple, onion, raisins, brown sugar, curry powder, poultry seasoning and garlic powder in large bowl. Toss with remaining ¾ cup apple juice.

**3.** Sprinkle crouton mixture over chicken; cover with foil. Bake 45 minutes or until chicken is no longer pink in center.

*Makes 4 servings*

# Classic Veg•All® Chicken Pot Pie

2 cans (15 ounces each) VEG•ALL®
  Original Mixed Vegetables,
  drained
1 can (10 ounces) cooked chicken,
  drained
1 can (10¾ ounces) condensed
  cream of chicken soup,
  undiluted
¼ teaspoon dried thyme
¼ teaspoon black pepper
2 (9-inch) frozen ready-to-bake
  pie crusts, thawed

Preheat oven to 375°F. In medium bowl, combine Veg•All, chicken, soup, thyme and pepper; mix well. Fit one pie crust into 9-inch pie pan; pour vegetable mixture into pie crust. Top with remaining crust; crimp edges to seal and prick top with fork.

Bake for 30 to 45 minutes (on lower rack) or until crust is golden brown and filling is hot. Allow pie to cool slightly before cutting into wedges to serve.

*Makes 4 servings*

# Spicy Chicken Casserole with Corn Bread

2 tablespoons olive oil
4 boneless skinless chicken breasts, cut into bite-size pieces
1 package (about 1 ounce) taco seasoning mix
1 can (about 15 ounces) black beans, rinsed and drained
1 can (about 14 ounces) diced tomatoes, drained
1 can (about 10 ounces) Mexican-style corn, drained
1 can (4 ounces) diced mild green chiles, drained
½ cup mild salsa
1 package (about 8 ounces) corn bread mix, plus ingredients to
    prepare mix
½ cup (2 ounces) shredded Cheddar cheese
¼ cup chopped red bell pepper

**1.** Preheat oven to 350°F. Spray 2-quart casserole with nonstick cooking spray. Heat oil in large skillet over medium heat. Add chicken; cook and stir 3 to 4 minutes or until cooked through.

**2.** Sprinkle taco seasoning over chicken. Add beans, tomatoes, corn, chiles and salsa; stir until well blended. Transfer to prepared casserole.

**3.** Prepare corn bread mix according to package directions, adding cheese and bell pepper to batter. Spread batter over chicken mixture. Bake 30 minutes or until corn bread is golden brown.

*Makes 4 to 6 servings*

# Chicken-Asparagus Casserole

    2 teaspoons vegetable oil
    1 cup diced green and/or red bell peppers
    1 medium onion, chopped
    2 cloves garlic, minced
    1 can (10¾ ounces) condensed cream of asparagus soup, undiluted
    1 container (8 ounces) ricotta cheese
    2 cups (8 ounces) shredded Cheddar cheese, divided
    2 eggs
 1½ cups chopped cooked chicken
    1 package (10 ounces) frozen chopped asparagus,* thawed and
        drained
    8 ounces egg noodles, cooked and drained
        Black pepper (optional)

*Or substitute ½ pound fresh asparagus cut into ½-inch pieces. Bring 6 cups water to a boil over high heat in large saucepan. Add fresh asparagus. Reduce heat to medium. Cover and cook 5 to 8 minutes or until crisp-tender. Drain.*

**1.** Preheat oven to 350°F. Grease 13×9-inch casserole. Heat oil in medium skillet over medium heat. Add bell peppers, onion and garlic; cook and stir until vegetables are crisp-tender.

**2.** Mix soup, ricotta cheese, 1 cup Cheddar cheese and eggs in large bowl until well blended. Add onion mixture, chicken, asparagus and noodles; mix well. Season with pepper, if desired.

**3.** Spread mixture evenly in prepared casserole. Top with remaining 1 cup Cheddar cheese. Bake 30 minutes or until center is set and cheese is bubbly. Let stand 5 minutes before serving.          *Makes 12 servings*

# Bayou-Style Pot Pie

    1 tablespoon olive oil
    1 large onion, chopped
    1 green bell pepper, diced
 1½ teaspoons minced garlic
  ½ pound boneless skinless chicken thighs, cut into 1-inch pieces
    1 can (about 14 ounces) stewed tomatoes
  ½ pound fully cooked smoked sausage or kielbasa, thinly sliced
  ¾ teaspoon hot pepper sauce, or to taste
2¼ cups buttermilk biscuit baking mix
  ¾ teaspoon dried thyme
  ⅛ teaspoon black pepper
  ⅔ cup milk

**1.** Preheat oven to 450°F. Heat oil in medium ovenproof skillet over medium-high heat. Add onion, bell pepper and garlic; cook and stir 3 minutes.

**2.** Add chicken; cook and stir 1 minute. Add tomatoes, sausage and hot pepper sauce. Cook, uncovered, over medium-low heat 5 minutes or until chicken is cooked through.

**3.** Meanwhile, combine baking mix, thyme and black pepper in medium bowl. Stir in milk. Drop batter by heaping tablespoonfuls over chicken mixture. Bake 14 minutes or until biscuits are golden brown and cooked through and chicken mixture is bubbly.    *Makes 4 servings*

**Note:** You can use any variety of fully cooked sausages from your supermarket meat case. Andouille, a fairly spicy Louisiana-style sausage, is perfect for this dish.

Prep and Cook Time: 28 minutes

# Artichoke-Olive Chicken Bake

1½ **cups uncooked rotini pasta**
1 **tablespoon olive oil**
1 **medium onion, chopped**
½ **green bell pepper, diced**
2 **cups shredded cooked chicken**
1 **can (about 14 ounces) diced tomatoes with Italian herbs**
1 **can (14 ounces) artichoke hearts, drained and quartered**
1 **can (6 ounces) sliced black olives, drained**
1 **teaspoon Italian seasoning**
2 **cups (8 ounces) shredded mozzarella cheese**

**1.** Preheat oven to 350°F. Spray 2-quart casserole with nonstick cooking spray. Cook pasta according to package directions until al dente; drain.

**2.** Heat oil in large deep skillet over medium heat. Add onion and bell pepper; cook and stir 1 minute. Add pasta, chicken, tomatoes, artichokes, olives and Italian seasoning; mix until blended.

**3.** Place half of chicken mixture in prepared casserole; sprinkle with half of cheese. Top with remaining chicken mixture and cheese. Bake, covered, 35 minutes or until hot and bubbly. *Makes 8 servings*

# Chicken Normandy Style

2 tablespoons butter, divided
3 cups peeled, thinly sliced apples, such as Fuji or Braeburn (about
    3 apples)
1 pound ground chicken
¼ cup apple brandy or apple juice
1 can (10¾ ounces) condensed cream of chicken soup, undiluted
¼ cup chopped green onions
2 teaspoons minced fresh sage leaves *or* ½ teaspoon dried sage
¼ teaspoon black pepper
1 package (12 ounces) egg noodles, cooked and drained

**1.** Preheat oven to 350°F. Grease 9-inch square casserole. Melt
1 tablespoon butter in large nonstick skillet. Add apples; cook and stir
over medium heat 7 to 10 minutes or until tender. Remove apples from
skillet.

**2.** Brown chicken in same skillet over medium heat, stirring to break up
meat. Stir in brandy; cook 2 minutes. Stir in soup, green onions, sage,
pepper and apple slices. Reduce heat; simmer 5 minutes.

**3.** Melt remaining 1 tablespoon butter and toss with noodles. Spoon into
prepared casserole. Top with chicken mixture. Bake 15 minutes or until
hot and bubbly. *Makes 4 servings*

# Great Grilling

## Blue Cheese Stuffed Chicken Breasts

½ cup (2 ounces) crumbled blue cheese
2 tablespoons butter, softened, divided
¾ teaspoon dried thyme
  Salt and black pepper
4 bone-in chicken breasts with skin
1 tablespoon lemon juice
½ teaspoon paprika

**1.** Spray cold grid with nonstick cooking spray. Prepare grill for direct cooking. Combine blue cheese, 1 tablespoon butter and thyme in small bowl until blended. Season with salt and pepper.

**2.** Loosen skin over chicken by pushing fingers between skin and meat, taking care not to tear skin. Spread blue cheese mixture under skin; massage skin to evenly spread cheese mixture.

**3.** Place chicken, skin side down, on grid over medium coals. Grill, covered, 15 minutes. Meanwhile, melt remaining 1 tablespoon butter in small bowl; stir in lemon juice and paprika. Turn chicken; brush with lemon juice mixture. Grill 15 to 20 minutes more or until chicken is cooked through (165°F). *Makes 4 servings*

**Serving Suggestion:** Serve with steamed new potatoes and broccoli.

Prep and Cook Time: 40 minutes

# Grilled Rosemary Chicken

**2 tablespoons minced fresh rosemary leaves**
**2 tablespoons lemon juice**
**2 tablespoons olive oil**
**2 cloves garlic, minced**
**¼ teaspoon salt**
**4 boneless skinless chicken breasts**

**1.** Spray cold grid with nonstick cooking spray. Prepare grill for direct cooking.

**2.** Whisk together rosemary, lemon juice, oil, garlic and salt in small bowl. Pour into shallow glass dish. Add chicken, turning to coat both sides. Cover; marinate in refrigerator 15 minutes, turning chicken once.

**3.** Remove chicken from marinade; discard marinade. Grill chicken over medium-hot coals 5 to 6 minutes per side or until chicken is no longer pink in center. *Makes 4 servings*

**Note:** For added flavor, moisten a few sprigs of fresh rosemary and toss on the hot coals just before grilling.

**Tip:** To store fresh rosemary, wrap sprigs in a barely damp paper towel and place in a sealed food storage bag. It can be kept in the refrigerator for up to five days.

**Prep and Cook Time:** 30 minutes

# Thai Grilled Chicken

**4 boneless skinless chicken breasts**
**¼ cup low-sodium soy sauce**
**2 teaspoons minced garlic**
**½ teaspoon red pepper flakes**
**2 tablespoons honey**
**1 tablespoon fresh lime juice**

**1.** Spray cold grid with nonstick cooking spray. Prepare grill for direct cooking. Place chicken in shallow baking dish. Combine soy sauce, garlic and pepper flakes in small bowl. Pour over chicken, turning to coat. Let stand 10 minutes.

**2.** Meanwhile, whisk honey and lime juice in small bowl.

**3.** Place chicken on grid over medium coals; brush with marinade. Discard remaining marinade. Grill, covered, 5 minutes. Brush both sides of chicken with honey mixture. Grill 5 minutes more or until chicken is no longer pink in center.                    *Makes 4 servings*

**Serving Suggestion:** Serve with steamed white rice and grilled fruit.

Prep and Cook Time: 25 minutes

# Persian Chicken Breasts

1 medium lemon
2 teaspoons olive oil
1 teaspoon ground cinnamon
½ teaspoon salt
¼ teaspoon black pepper
¼ teaspoon turmeric
4 boneless skinless chicken
    breasts
4 flour tortillas or soft lavash
    (optional)
Grilled bell peppers (optional)

**1.** Juice lemon. Combine juice, oil, cinnamon, salt, pepper and turmeric in large resealable food storage bag. Gently knead ingredients in bag to mix thoroughly; add chicken. Seal bag; turn to coat. Marinate in refrigerator 4 hours or overnight.

**2.** Spray cold grid with nonstick cooking spray. Prepare grill for direct cooking. Remove chicken from marinade; gently shake to remove excess. Discard remaining marinade. Grill chicken over medium heat 5 to 7 minutes per side or until chicken is no longer pink in center.

**3.** Serve chicken with lightly grilled tortillas and bell peppers, if desired.

*Makes 4 servings*

# Grilled Chicken with Spicy Black Beans & Rice

**1 boneless skinless chicken breast**
**½ teaspoon Caribbean jerk seasoning**
**½ teaspoon olive oil**
**¼ cup finely diced green bell pepper**
**2 teaspoons chipotle chili powder**
**¾ cup hot cooked rice**
**½ cup rinsed and drained canned black beans**
**2 tablespoons diced pimiento**
**1 tablespoon chopped pimiento-stuffed green olives**
**1 tablespoon chopped onion**
**1 tablespoon chopped fresh cilantro (optional)**
**Lime wedges (optional)**

**1.** Spray cold grid with nonstick cooking spray. Prepare grill for direct cooking. Rub chicken with jerk seasoning. Grill chicken over medium heat 8 to 10 minutes or until no longer pink in center, turning once.

**2.** Meanwhile, heat oil in medium saucepan over medium heat. Add bell pepper and chili powder; cook and stir until peppers are tender. Add rice, beans, pimiento and olives; cook about 3 minutes or until heated through.

**3.** Slice chicken; arrange over rice mixture. Sprinkle with onion and cilantro, if desired. Garnish with lime wedges.       *Makes 2 servings*

# Lime-Mustard Marinated Chicken

**2 boneless skinless chicken breasts**
**¼ cup fresh lime juice**
**3 tablespoons honey mustard, divided**
**2 teaspoons olive oil**
**¼ teaspoon ground cumin**
**⅛ teaspoon garlic powder**
**⅛ teaspoon ground red pepper**
**¾ cup plus 2 tablespoons chicken broth, divided**
**¼ cup uncooked rice**
**1 cup broccoli florets**
**⅓ cup matchstick carrots**

**1.** Place chicken in large resealable food storage bag. Whisk together lime juice, 2 tablespoons mustard, oil, cumin, garlic powder and red pepper in small bowl. Pour mixture over chicken in bag. Seal bag; turn to coat. Marinate in refrigerator 2 hours.

**2.** Combine ¾ cup broth, rice and remaining 1 tablespoon mustard in small saucepan. Bring to a boil over high heat. Reduce heat; cover and simmer 12 minutes or until rice is almost tender. Stir in broccoli, carrots and remaining 2 tablespoons broth. Cook, covered, 2 to 3 minutes more or until vegetables are crisp-tender and rice is tender.

**3.** Spray cold grid with nonstick cooking spray. Prepare grill for direct cooking. Drain chicken; discard marinade. Grill chicken over medium heat, turning once, 10 to 13 minutes or until no longer pink in center. Serve chicken with rice mixture. *Makes 2 servings*

**Hint:** This marinade works well with other chicken cuts. Try boneless skinless thighs. They have a little more fat than breasts, so they tend to stay moist and tender.

# Grilled Chicken and Vegetable Kabobs

⅓ cup olive oil
¼ cup lemon juice
4 cloves garlic, coarsely chopped
½ teaspoon salt
½ teaspoon lemon pepper
½ teaspoon dried tarragon
1 pound chicken tenders
6 ounces mushrooms
1 cup sliced zucchini
½ cup cubed green bell pepper
½ cup cubed red bell pepper
1 red onion, quartered
6 cherry tomatoes
3 cups hot cooked rice

**1.** Combine oil, lemon juice, garlic, salt, lemon pepper and tarragon in large resealable food storage bag. Add chicken, mushrooms, zucchini, bell peppers, onion and tomatoes. Seal bag; turn to coat. Marinate in refrigerator at least 8 hours, turning occasionally.

**2.** Soak 6 (10-inch) wooden skewers in water 20 minutes. Spray cold grid with nonstick cooking spray. Prepare grill for direct cooking. Remove chicken and vegetables from marinade; discard marinade. Thread chicken and vegetables onto skewers.

**3.** Place skewers on grid. Grill, covered, over medium-hot coals 3 to 4 minutes on each side or until chicken is no longer pink in center. Remove chicken and vegetables from skewers. Serve over rice.

*Makes 6 servings*

# Ginger-Lime Chicken Thighs

⅓ **cup vegetable oil**
3 **tablespoons lime juice**
3 **tablespoons honey**
2 **teaspoons grated fresh ginger**
    *or* **1 teaspoon ground ginger**
¼ **to** ½ **teaspoon red pepper**
    **flakes**
6 **boneless skinless chicken thighs**

**1.** Combine oil, lime juice, honey, ginger and pepper flakes in small bowl. Place chicken in large resealable food storage bag. Add ½ cup marinade. Seal bag; turn to coat. Marinate in refrigerator 30 to 60 minutes, turning occasionally. Refrigerate remaining marinade.

**2.** Spray cold grid with nonstick cooking spray. Prepare grill for direct cooking.

**3.** Remove chicken from marinade; discard marinade. Place chicken on grid over medium-high heat. Grill chicken 12 minutes or until chicken is cooked through, turning once. Brush with refrigerated marinade during last 5 minutes of cooking.          *Makes 4 to 6 servings*

# Grilled Marinated Chicken

**8 whole chicken legs (thighs and
    drumsticks attached) (about
    3½ pounds)**
**6 ounces frozen lemonade
    concentrate, thawed**
**2 tablespoons white wine vinegar**
**1 tablespoon grated lemon peel**
**2 cloves garlic, minced**

**1.** Remove skin and all visible fat
from chicken. Place chicken in
13×9-inch glass baking dish.
Combine remaining ingredients in
small bowl; blend well. Pour over
chicken; turn to coat. Cover;
marinate in refrigerator 3 hours or
overnight, turning occasionally.

**2.** Spray cold grid with nonstick
cooking spray. Prepare grill for direct cooking.

**3.** Remove chicken from marinade; discard marinade. Place chicken on
grid over medium-hot coals. Grill 20 to 30 minutes or until chicken is
cooked through (165°F), turning occasionally.     *Makes 8 servings*

# Grilled Ginger Chicken with Pineapple and Coconut Rice

**1 can (20 ounces) pineapple slices in juice**
**⅔ cup uncooked rice**
**½ cup unsweetened flaked coconut**
**4 boneless skinless chicken breasts**
**1 tablespoon soy sauce**
**1 teaspoon ground ginger**

**1.** Drain juice from pineapple into glass measuring cup. Reserve 2 tablespoons juice. Combine remaining juice with enough water to equal 2 cups.

**2.** Cook and stir rice and coconut in medium saucepan over medium heat 3 to 4 minutes or until lightly browned. Add juice mixture; cover and bring to a boil. Reduce heat to low; cook 15 minutes or until rice is tender and liquid is absorbed.

**3.** Meanwhile, spray cold grid with nonstick cooking spray. Prepare grill for direct cooking. Combine chicken, reserved 2 tablespoons juice, soy sauce and ginger in medium bowl; toss to coat. Grill chicken over medium heat 6 minutes; turn. Add pineapple to grill. Cook 6 to 8 minutes or until chicken is no longer pink in center, turning pineapple after 3 minutes. Serve chicken with rice and pineapple.                *Makes 4 servings*

Prep and Cook Time: 22 minutes

# Spicy Island Chicken

    1 cup finely chopped onion
   ⅓ cup white wine vinegar
    6 green onions, finely chopped
    6 cloves garlic, minced
    1 habañero or serrano pepper,* finely chopped
 4½ teaspoons olive oil
 4½ teaspoons fresh thyme *or* 2 teaspoons dried thyme
    1 tablespoon ground allspice
    2 teaspoons sugar
    1 teaspoon salt
    1 teaspoon ground cinnamon
    1 teaspoon ground nutmeg
    1 teaspoon black pepper
   ½ teaspoon ground red pepper
    6 boneless skinless chicken breasts

*\*Habañero and serrano peppers can sting and irritate the skin, so wear rubber gloves when handling peppers and do not touch your eyes.*

**1.** Combine all ingredients except chicken in medium bowl; mix well. Place chicken in resealable food storage bag and add seasoning mixture. Seal bag; turn to coat chicken. Marinate in refrigerator 4 hours or overnight.

**2.** Spray cold grid with nonstick cooking spray. Prepare grill for direct cooking.

**3.** Remove chicken from marinade, reserving marinade. Grill chicken over medium-high heat 5 to 7 minutes per side or until chicken is no longer pink in center, brushing occasionally with marinade. *Do not brush with marinade during last 5 minutes of grilling.* Discard remaining marinade.       *Makes 6 servings*

**Serving Suggestion:** Serve with grilled sweet potatoes.

# Weeknight Meals

## Roast Chicken with Peppers

 1 chicken (3 to 3½ pounds), cut into pieces
 3 tablespoons olive oil, divided
 1 tablespoon plus 1½ teaspoons chopped fresh rosemary leaves *or*
     1½ teaspoons dried rosemary
 1 tablespoon fresh lemon juice
 1¼ teaspoons salt, divided
 ¾ teaspoon black pepper, divided
 3 bell peppers (red, yellow and/or green)
 1 medium onion

**1.** Preheat oven to 375°F. Place chicken in shallow roasting pan.

**2.** Combine 2 tablespoons oil, rosemary and lemon juice in small bowl; brush over chicken. Sprinkle 1 teaspoon salt and ½ teaspoon pepper over chicken. Roast chicken 15 minutes.

**3.** Cut bell peppers lengthwise into ½-inch-thick strips. Cut onion into thin wedges. Toss vegetables with remaining 1 tablespoon oil, ¼ teaspoon salt and ¼ teaspoon pepper in medium bowl. Spoon vegetables around chicken; roast about 40 minutes or until vegetables are tender and chicken is cooked through (165°F). Serve chicken with vegetables and pan juices. *Makes 6 servings*

# Greek Chicken

**12 cloves garlic, unpeeled**
**3 pounds chicken leg and thigh pieces**
**4 tablespoons lemon juice, divided**
**3 tablespoons olive oil**
**2 tablespoons chopped fresh rosemary leaves *or* 2 teaspoons dried rosemary**
**¾ teaspoon salt**
**½ teaspoon black pepper**
**1 teaspoon grated lemon peel**
**Additional sprigs fresh rosemary and lemon wedges (optional)**

**1.** Preheat oven to 375°F. Arrange garlic in shallow roasting pan. Place chicken over garlic. Combine 2 tablespoons lemon juice, oil and rosemary in small bowl; spoon evenly over chicken. Sprinkle chicken with salt and pepper.

**2.** Bake 50 to 55 minutes or until chicken is cooked through (165°F). Transfer chicken to serving platter; keep warm.

**3.** Squeeze garlic pulp from skins; discard skins. Place garlic pulp in roasting pan; add remaining 2 tablespoons lemon juice. Cook over medium heat, mashing garlic and stirring to scrape up browned bits. Pour sauce over chicken; sprinkle with lemon peel. Garnish with rosemary sprigs and lemon wedges. *Makes 4 servings*

**Hint:** Add more lemon to taste. Tuck a few lemon wedges or slices among the chicken pieces before roasting.

**Tip:** Unpeeled cloves of garlic usually burst open while roasting, making it a cinch to squeeze out the softened, creamy roasted garlic with your thumb and forefinger. If the cloves have not burst open, simply slice off the end with a knife and squeeze out the garlic.

# Continental Chicken

**1 package (2¼ ounces) dried beef, cut into pieces**
**4 boneless skinless chicken breasts**
**4 slices bacon**
**1 can (10¾ ounces) condensed cream of mushroom soup, undiluted**
**¼ cup all-purpose flour**
**¼ cup sour cream**
   **Hot cooked noodles**

### SLOW COOKER DIRECTIONS

**1.** Spray slow cooker with nonstick cooking spray. Place dried beef in slow cooker. Wrap each piece of chicken with 1 bacon slice. Place wrapped chicken on top of dried beef.

**2.** Combine soup and flour in medium bowl until smooth. Pour over chicken.

**3.** Cover; cook on LOW 7 to 8 hours or on HIGH 3 to 4 hours. Place sour cream in small bowl; stir in a few tablespoons of juices from slow cooker. Stir sour cream mixture into slow cooker. Cook 5 minutes or until heated through. Serve over noodles.          *Makes 4 servings*

# Quick Chicken Jambalaya

   **8 boneless skinless chicken thighs, cut into bite-size pieces**
   **¼ teaspoon garlic salt**
   **1 tablespoon vegetable oil**
**2½ cups 8-vegetable juice**
   **1 bag (16 ounces) frozen pepper stir-fry mix**
   **½ cup diced cooked ham**
   **1 teaspoon hot pepper sauce**
**1¾ cups uncooked quick cooking rice**

Sprinkle chicken with garlic salt. In large nonstick skillet, place oil and heat over medium-high heat. Add chicken and cook, stirring occasionally, 8 minutes or until chicken is lightly browned. Add vegetable juice, pepper stir-fry mix, ham and hot pepper sauce. Heat to boiling; cover and cook over medium heat 4 minutes. Stir in rice; heat to boiling. Cover; remove pan from heat and let stand 5 minutes or until rice and vegetables are tender and liquid is absorbed.

*Makes 4 servings*

Favorite recipe from **Delmarva Poultry Industry, Inc.**

# Crispy Buttermilk Fried Chicken

**2 cups buttermilk**
**1 tablespoon hot pepper sauce**
**3 pounds bone-in chicken pieces**
**2 cups all-purpose flour**
**2 teaspoons salt**
**2 teaspoons poultry seasoning**
**1 teaspoon garlic salt**
**1 teaspoon paprika**
**1 teaspoon ground red pepper**
**1 teaspoon black pepper**
**1 cup vegetable oil**

**1.** Combine buttermilk and hot pepper sauce in large resealable food storage bag. Add chicken; seal bag. Turn to coat; marinate in refrigerator 2 hours or up to 24 hours.

**2.** Combine flour, salt, poultry seasoning, garlic salt, paprika, red pepper and black pepper in another large food storage bag or shallow baking dish; blend well. Working in batches, remove chicken from buttermilk; shake off excess. Add to flour mixture; shake to coat.

**3.** Heat oil over medium heat in deep heavy skillet until 350°F on deep-fry thermometer. Fry chicken in batches 30 minutes or until cooked through (165°F), turning occasionally to brown all sides. Drain on paper towels. *Makes 4 servings*

**Note:** Carefully monitor the temperature of the oil during cooking. It should not drop below 325°F or go higher than 350°F. The chicken can also be cooked in a deep fryer following the manufacturer's directions. Never leave hot oil unattended.

**Prep Time:** 15 minutes • **Cook Time:** 30 minutes • **Marinate Time:** 2 to 24 hours

# Tropical Chicken Salad Pockets

**3 cups diced cooked chicken***
**1 can (20 ounces) pineapple chunks in juice, drained, juice reserved**
**3 green onions, thinly sliced**
**2 tablespoons chopped fresh cilantro**
  **Tropical Dressing (recipe follows)**
**4 pocket breads, split**
  **Lettuce leaves**

*\*Use home-roasted chicken or ready-to-eat roasted chicken from the supermarket or deli.*

In bowl, place chicken, pineapple, green onions and cilantro. Pour dressing over chicken mixture and toss to mix. Line each pocket bread with lettuce leaf; fill with chicken salad. *Makes 4 servings*

**Tropical Dressing:** In small bowl, mix together ½ cup reduced-fat mayonnaise, 1 tablespoon lime juice, 1 tablespoon reserved pineapple juice, 1 teaspoon sugar, 1 teaspoon curry powder, ½ teaspoon salt and ¼ teaspoon grated lime peel. Makes about ⅔ cup dressing.

Favorite recipe from **Delmarva Poultry Industry, Inc.**

# Orange Pecan Chicken

1 cup orange juice
¼ cup vegetable oil
  Salt and black pepper
4 boneless skinless chicken breasts
  Orange Pecan Sauce (recipe follows)

**1.** Whisk together juice and oil in medium bowl until well blended. Season with salt and pepper. Place chicken in resealable food storage bag. Pour juice mixture over chicken. Seal bag; turn to coat. Marinate in refrigerator 30 minutes.

**2.** Prepare Orange Pecan Sauce.

**3.** Preheat broiler. Remove chicken from bag; discard marinade. Broil chicken 6 to 8 minutes on each side or until no longer pink in center, turning once. Serve with Orange Pecan Sauce.          *Makes 4 servings*

## Orange Pecan Sauce

⅓ cup frozen orange juice concentrate, thawed
⅓ cup butter
2 tablespoons teriyaki sauce
1 clove garlic, minced
2 tablespoons packed dark brown sugar
2 tablespoons chopped toasted pecans
  Dash ground red pepper

Combine orange juice concentrate, butter, teriyaki sauce and garlic in small saucepan. Bring to a simmer over medium heat. Cook and stir 2 to 3 minutes or until well blended. Add brown sugar. Cook and stir 4 to 5 minutes or until sauce is slightly thickened. Remove from heat. Stir in pecans and red pepper. Serve warm or at room temperature over chicken.          *Makes about 1 cup*

# Herbed Chicken and Vegetables

¾ teaspoon dried oregano, divided
1 teaspoon paprika
¼ teaspoon salt
⅛ teaspoon black pepper
2 skinless bone-in chicken breasts
2 sheets (18×12 inches each) heavy-duty foil
½ cup pasta sauce
½ medium green bell pepper, cut into squares
½ medium yellow bell pepper, cut into squares
½ cup chopped fresh mushrooms
¼ cup chopped onion
4 cloves garlic, minced
   Parmesan cheese
   Hot cooked egg noodles

**1.** Preheat oven to 450°F. Combine ½ teaspoon oregano, paprika, salt and pepper in small bowl; mix well. Lightly spray foil with nonstick cooking spray. Place chicken on foil sheets. Sprinkle chicken evenly with oregano mixture. Combine pasta sauce, bell peppers, mushrooms, onion, garlic and remaining ¼ teaspoon oregano in medium bowl. Pour evenly over chicken.

**2.** Double foil sides and ends of foil to seal packets, leaving head space for heat circulation. Place packets on baking sheet.

**3.** Bake 23 to 25 minutes or until chicken is cooked through (165°F). Carefully open ends of packets to allow steam to escape. Open packets and transfer contents to serving plates. Sprinkle with Parmesan cheese. Serve with noodles. *Makes 2 servings*

## 140 • Index

# *Acknowledgments*

*The publisher would like to thank the companies and organizations listed below for the use of their recipes and photographs in this publication.*

Delmarva Poultry Industry, Inc.

Dole Food Company, Inc.

Pacific Northwest Canned Pear Service

Veg•All®

# METRIC CONVERSION CHART

## VOLUME MEASUREMENTS (dry)

$1/8$ teaspoon = 0.5 mL
$1/4$ teaspoon = 1 mL
$1/2$ teaspoon = 2 mL
$3/4$ teaspoon = 4 mL
1 teaspoon = 5 mL
1 tablespoon = 15 mL
2 tablespoons = 30 mL
$1/4$ cup = 60 mL
$1/3$ cup = 75 mL
$1/2$ cup = 125 mL
$2/3$ cup = 150 mL
$3/4$ cup = 175 mL
1 cup = 250 mL
2 cups = 1 pint = 500 mL
3 cups = 750 mL
4 cups = 1 quart = 1 L

## VOLUME MEASUREMENTS (fluid)

1 fluid ounce (2 tablespoons) = 30 mL
4 fluid ounces ($1/2$ cup) = 125 mL
8 fluid ounces (1 cup) = 250 mL
12 fluid ounces ($1 1/2$ cups) = 375 mL
16 fluid ounces (2 cups) = 500 mL

## WEIGHTS (mass)

$1/2$ ounce = 15 g
1 ounce = 30 g
3 ounces = 90 g
4 ounces = 120 g
8 ounces = 225 g
10 ounces = 285 g
12 ounces = 360 g
16 ounces = 1 pound = 450 g

## DIMENSIONS

$1/16$ inch = 2 mm
$1/8$ inch = 3 mm
$1/4$ inch = 6 mm
$1/2$ inch = 1.5 cm
$3/4$ inch = 2 cm
1 inch = 2.5 cm

## OVEN TEMPERATURES

250°F = 120°C
275°F = 140°C
300°F = 150°C
325°F = 160°C
350°F = 180°C
375°F = 190°C
400°F = 200°C
425°F = 220°C
450°F = 230°C

## BAKING PAN SIZES

| Utensil | Size in Inches/Quarts | Metric Volume | Size in Centimeters |
|---|---|---|---|
| Baking or | $8 \times 8 \times 2$ | 2 L | $20 \times 20 \times 5$ |
| Cake Pan | $9 \times 9 \times 2$ | 2.5 L | $23 \times 23 \times 5$ |
| (square or | $12 \times 8 \times 2$ | 3 L | $30 \times 20 \times 5$ |
| rectangular) | $13 \times 9 \times 2$ | 3.5 L | $33 \times 23 \times 5$ |
| Loaf Pan | $8 \times 4 \times 3$ | 1.5 L | $20 \times 10 \times 7$ |
|  | $9 \times 5 \times 3$ | 2 L | $23 \times 13 \times 7$ |
| Round Layer | $8 \times 1 1/2$ | 1.2 L | $20 \times 4$ |
| Cake Pan | $9 \times 1 1/2$ | 1.5 L | $23 \times 4$ |
| Pie Plate | $8 \times 1 1/4$ | 750 mL | $20 \times 3$ |
|  | $9 \times 1 1/4$ | 1 L | $23 \times 3$ |
| Baking Dish | 1 quart | 1 L | — |
| or Casserole | $1 1/2$ quart | 1.5 L | — |
|  | 2 quart | 2 L | — |